Celtic Wildlife

Coloring Book

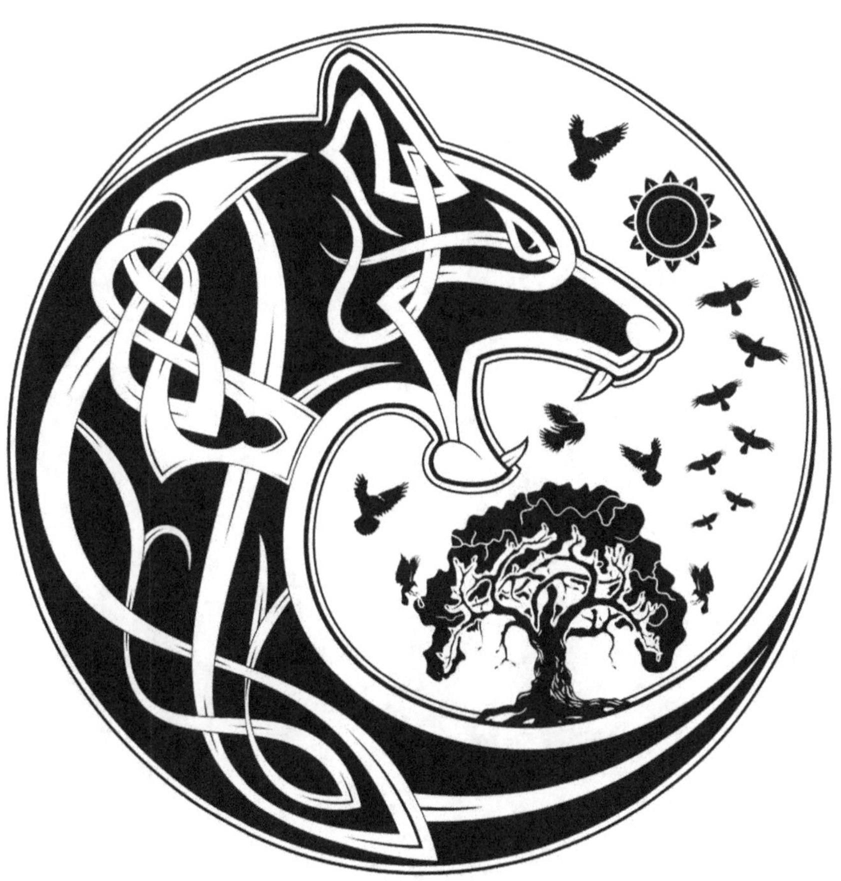

Relaxatio Amn

Thank you for choosing Relaxatio Amn
This coloring book made with love .

enjoy
it all.

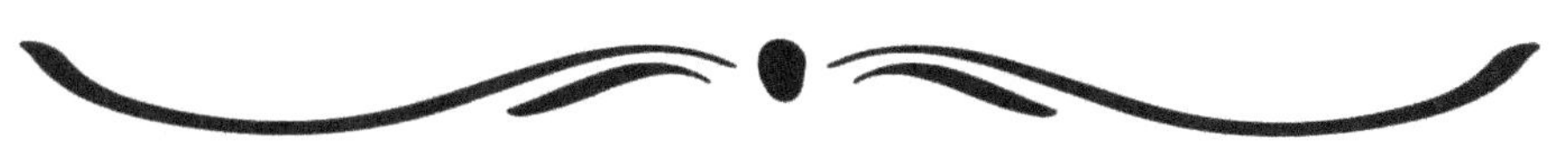

This Book Belong to

Name : …………………………………

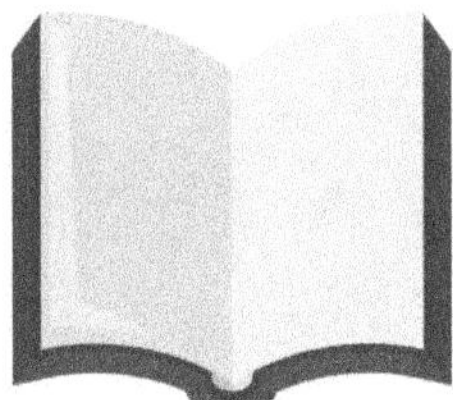

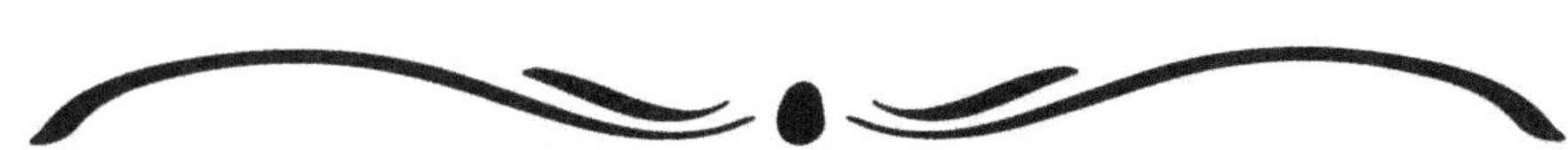

Color Test

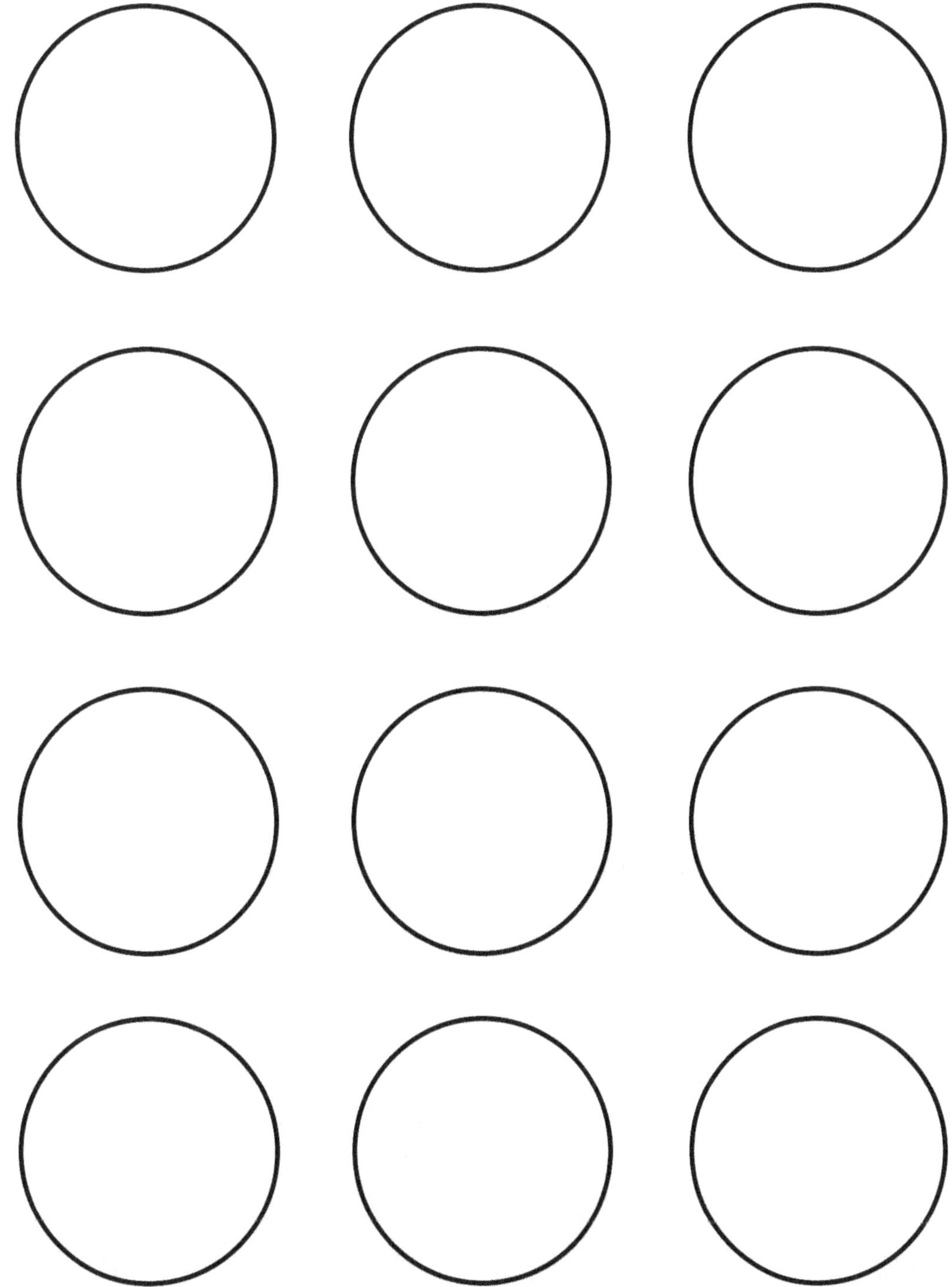

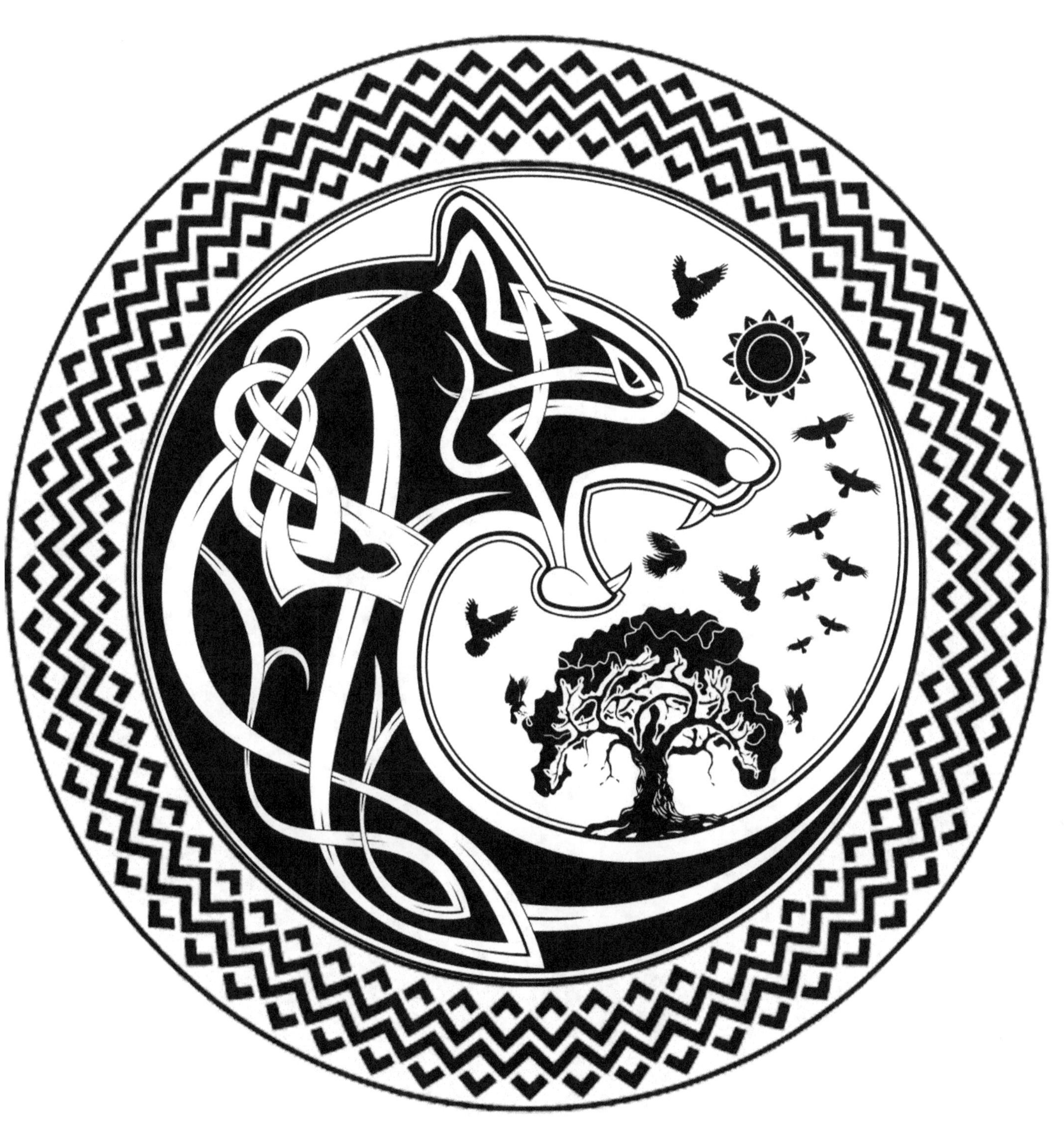

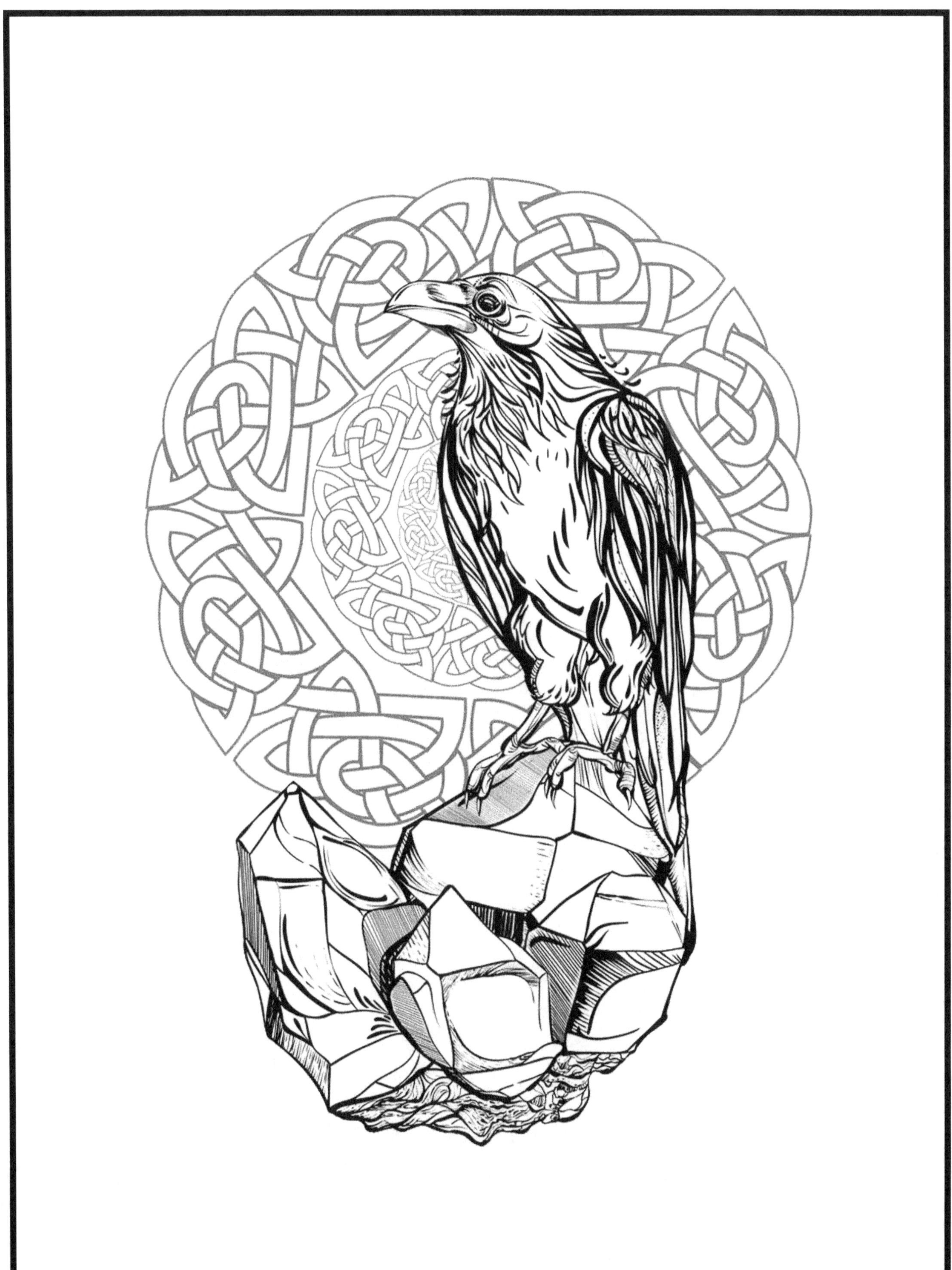

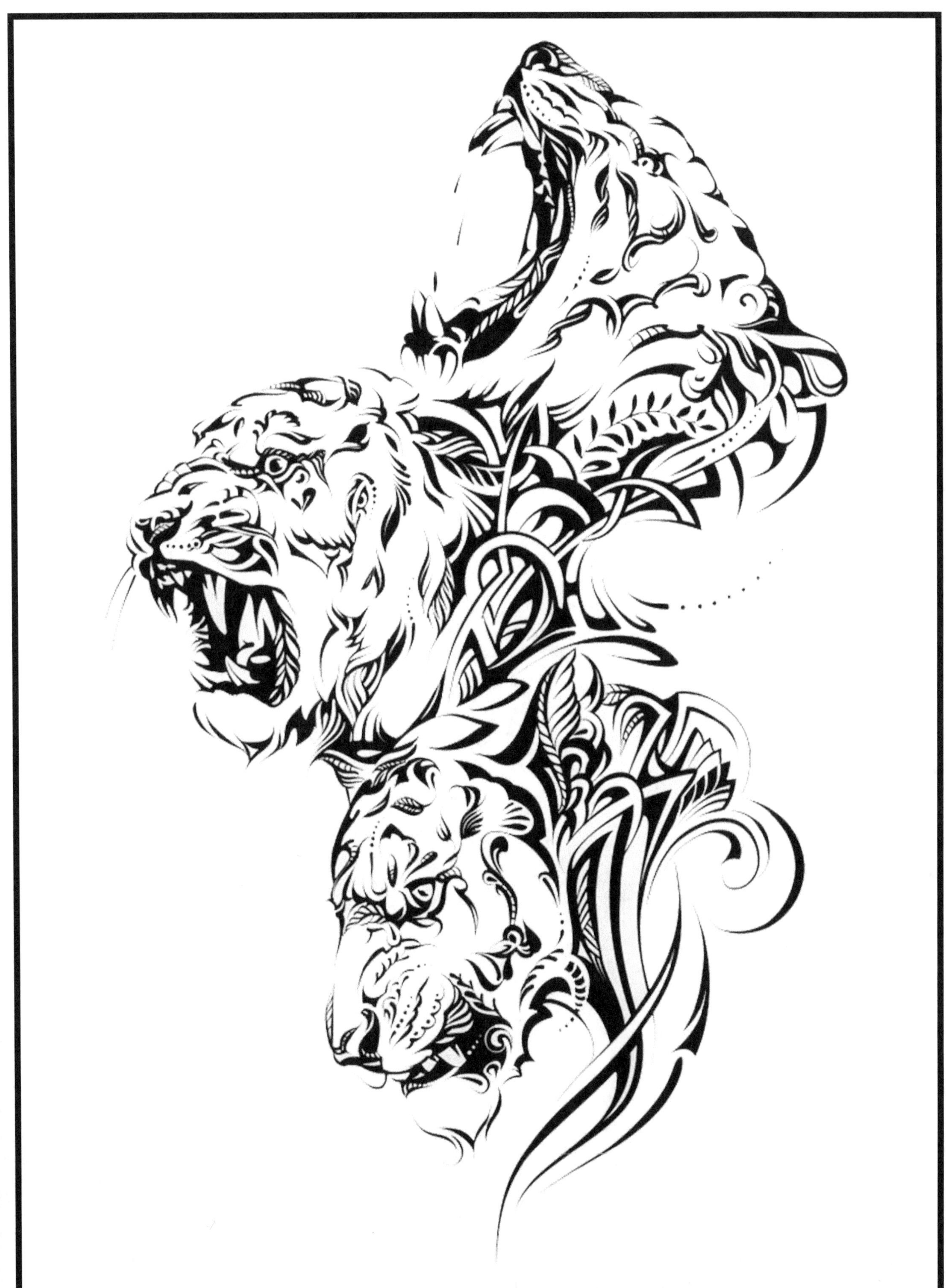

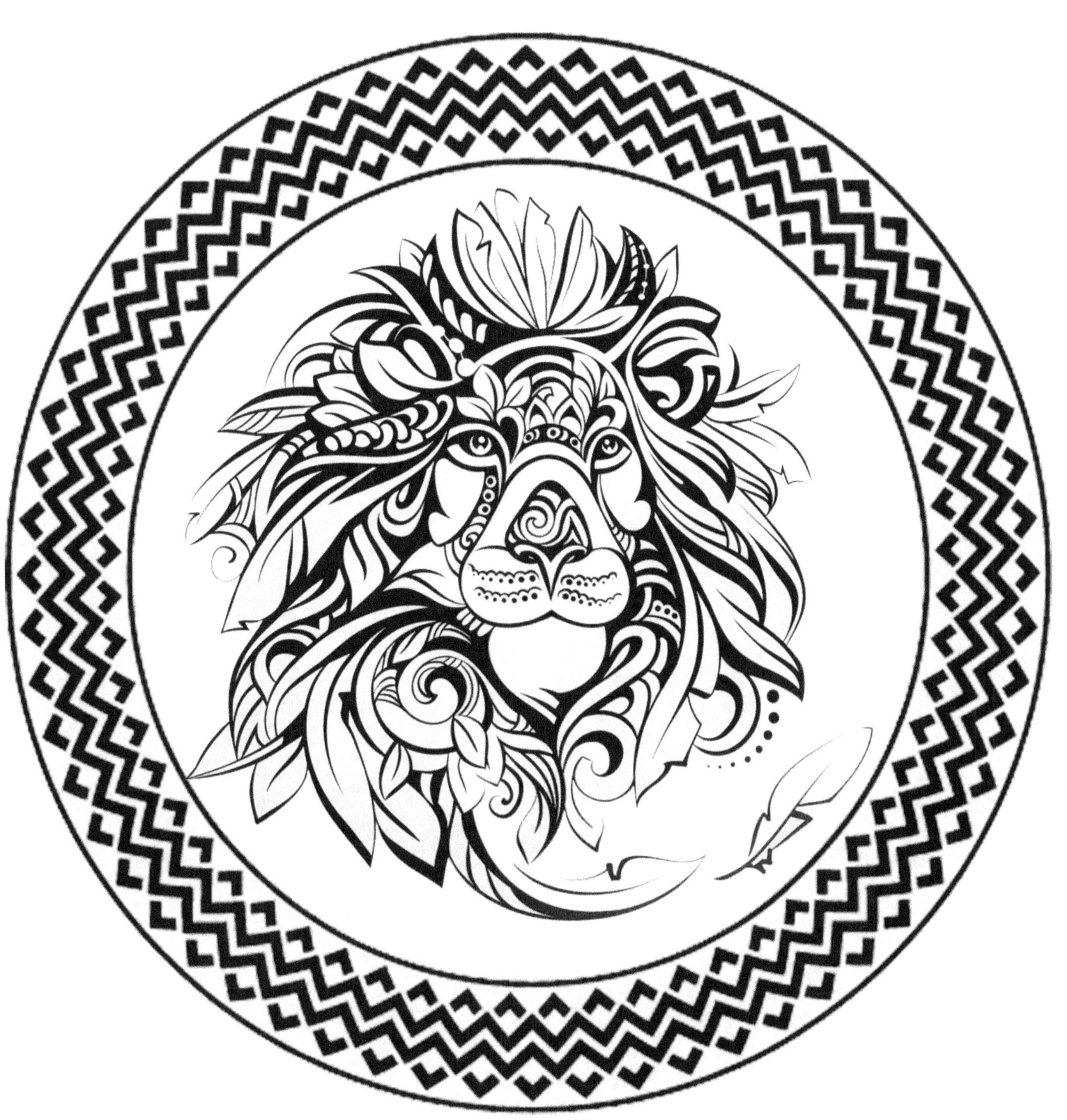

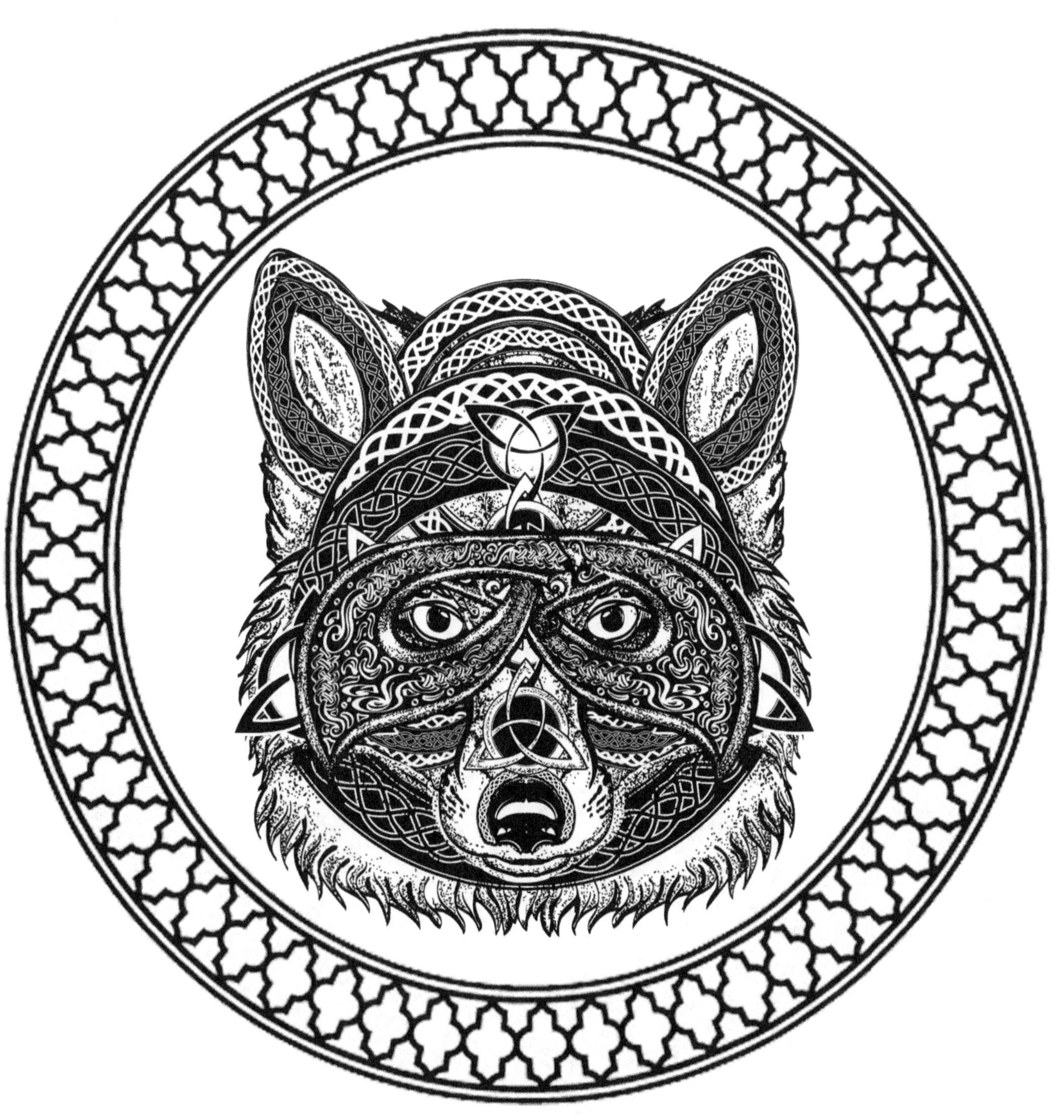

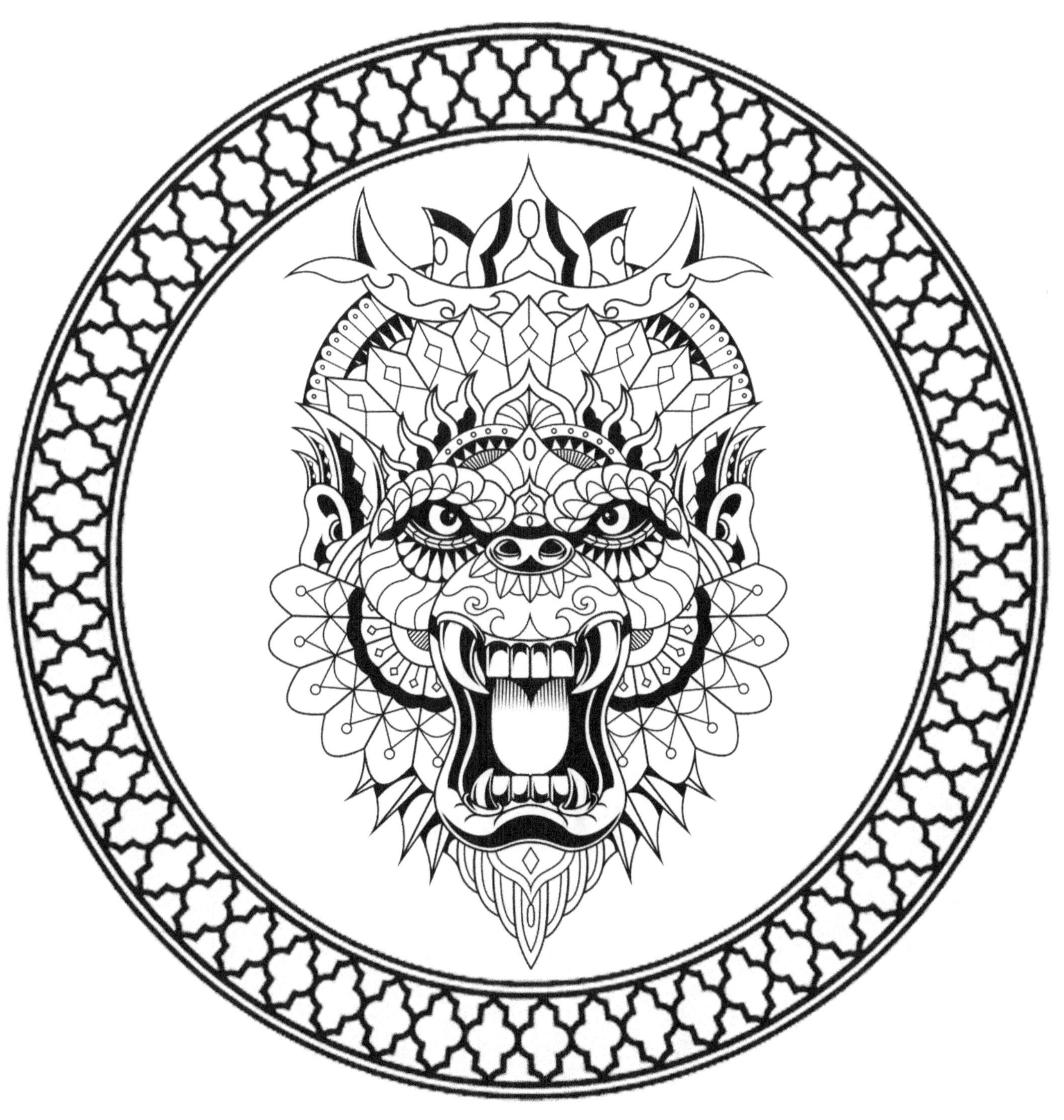

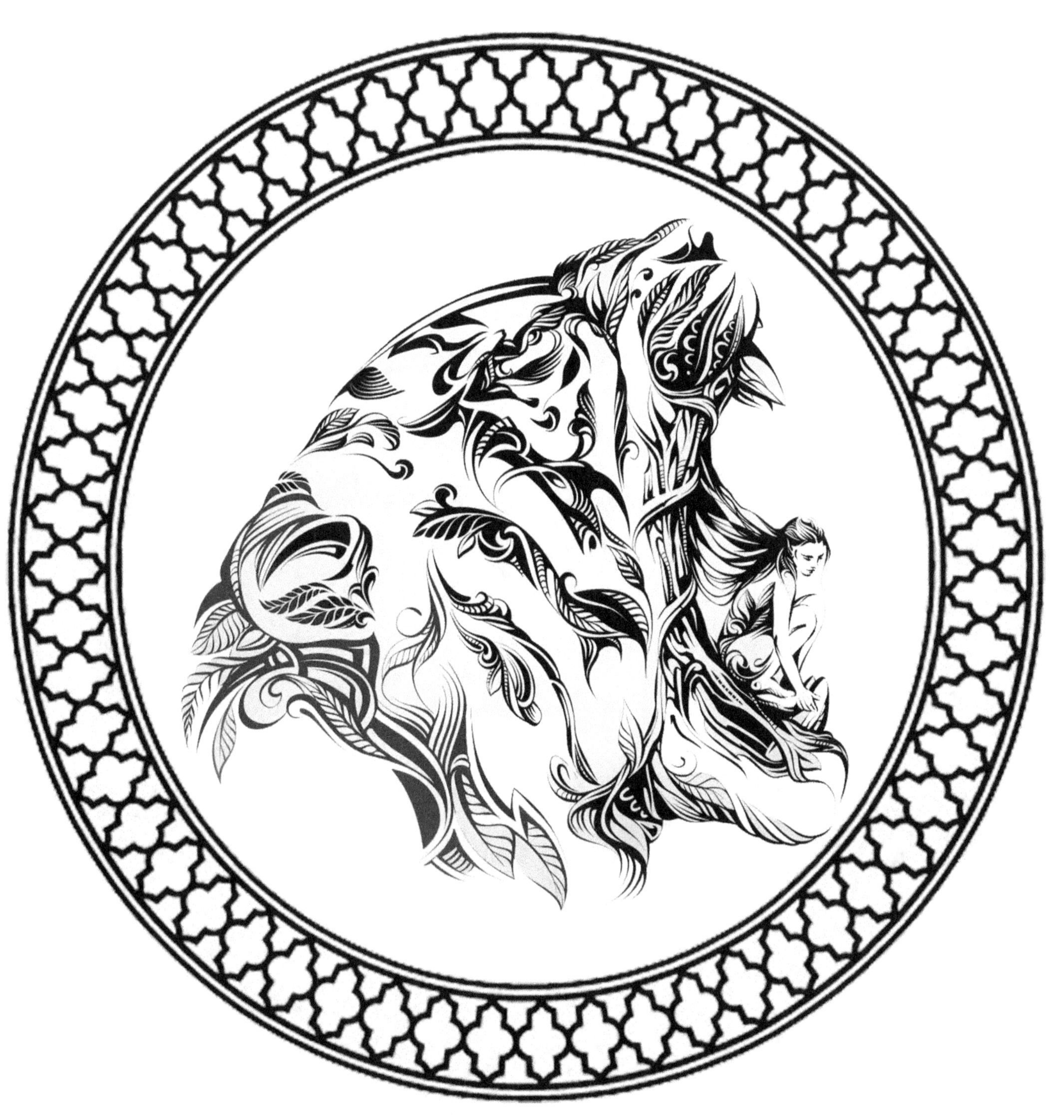

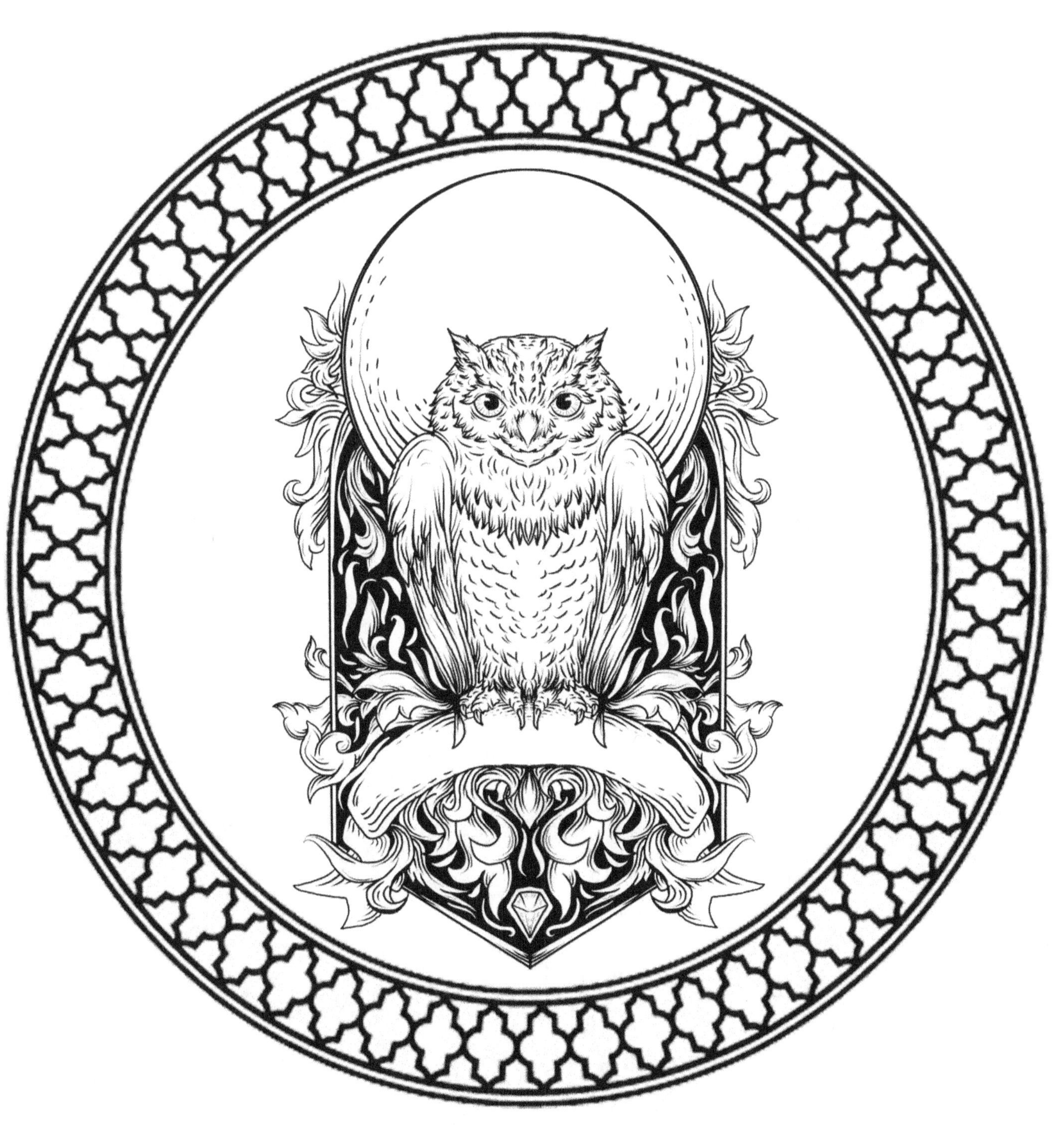

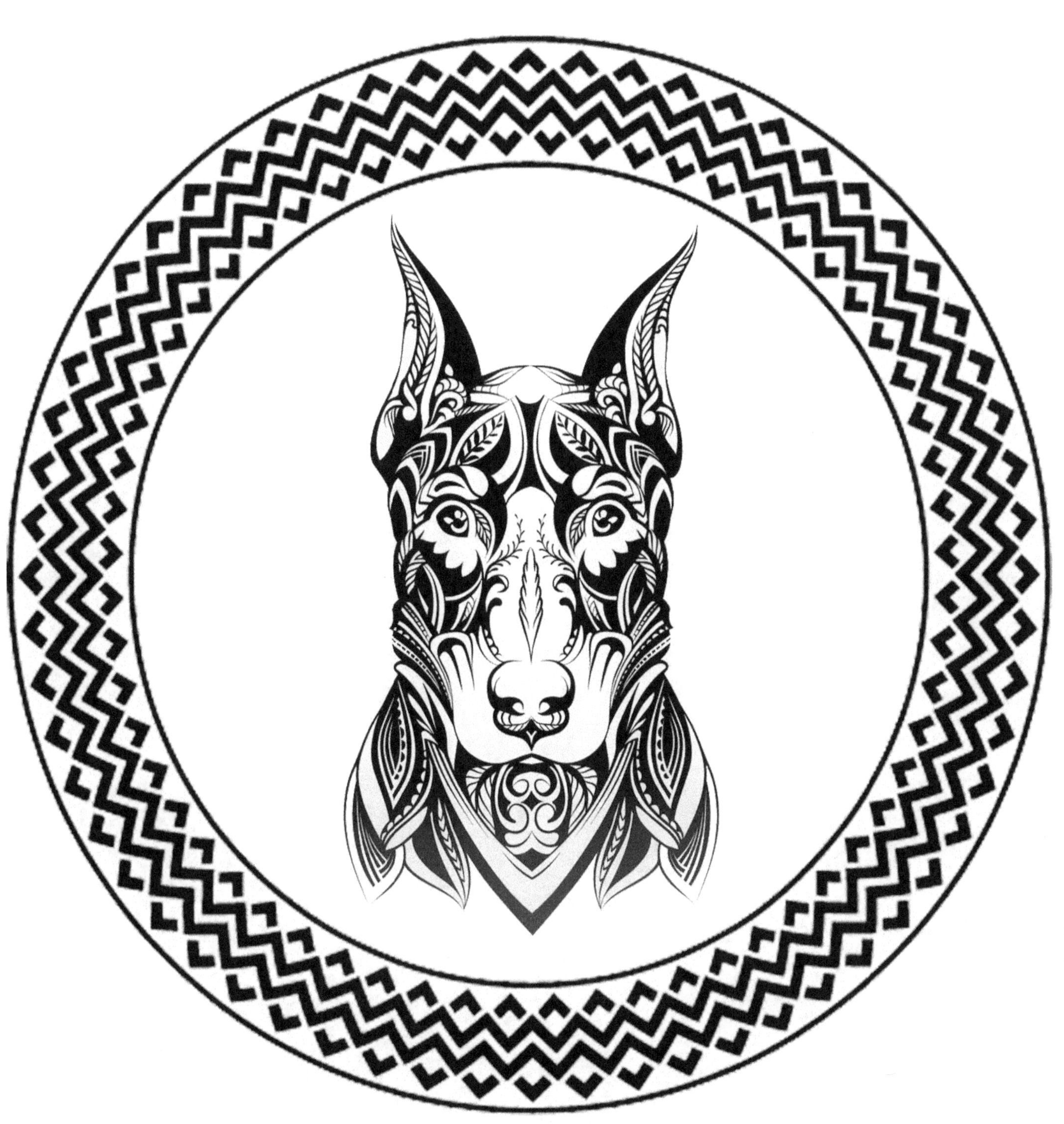

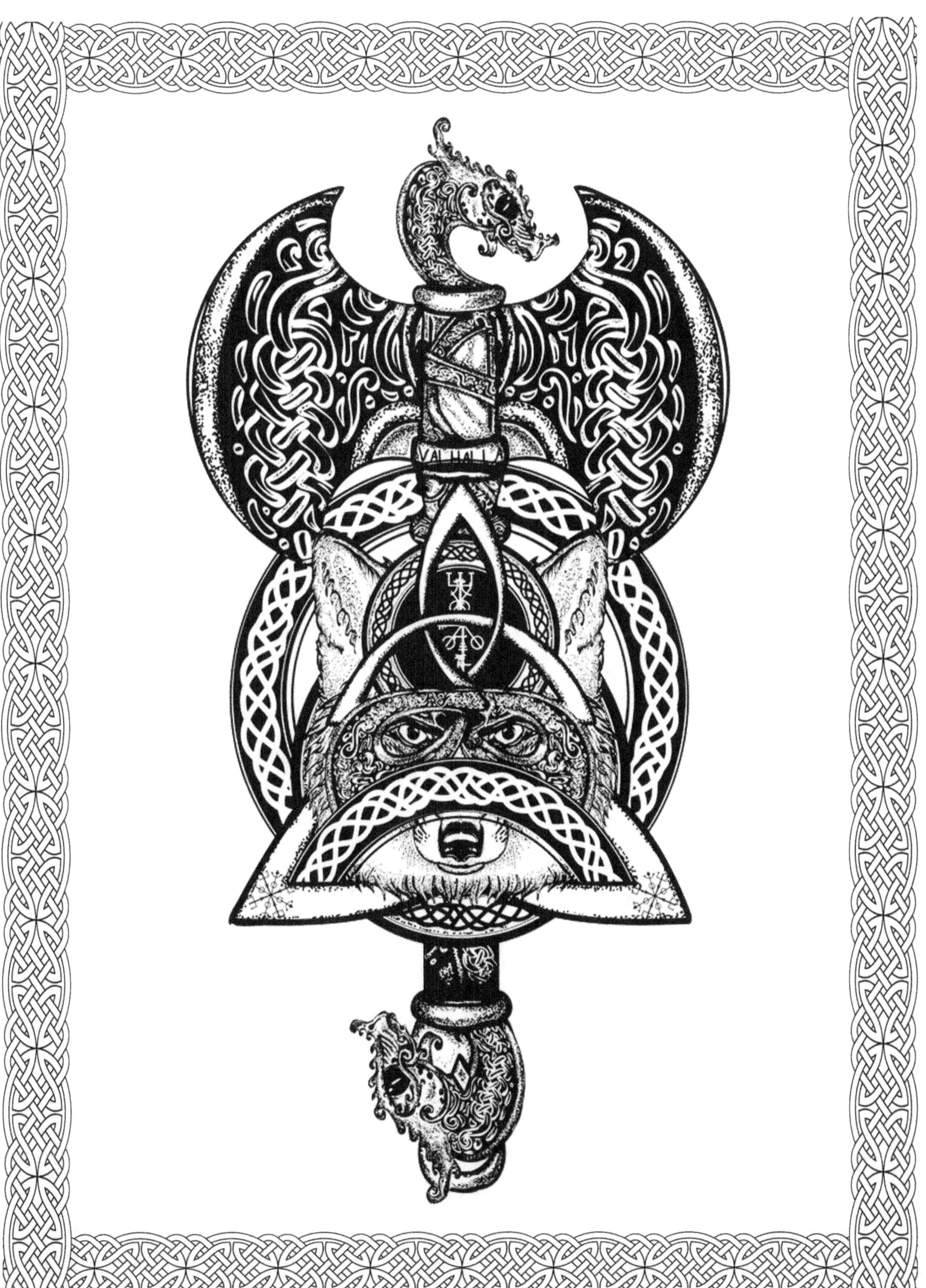
VALHALL

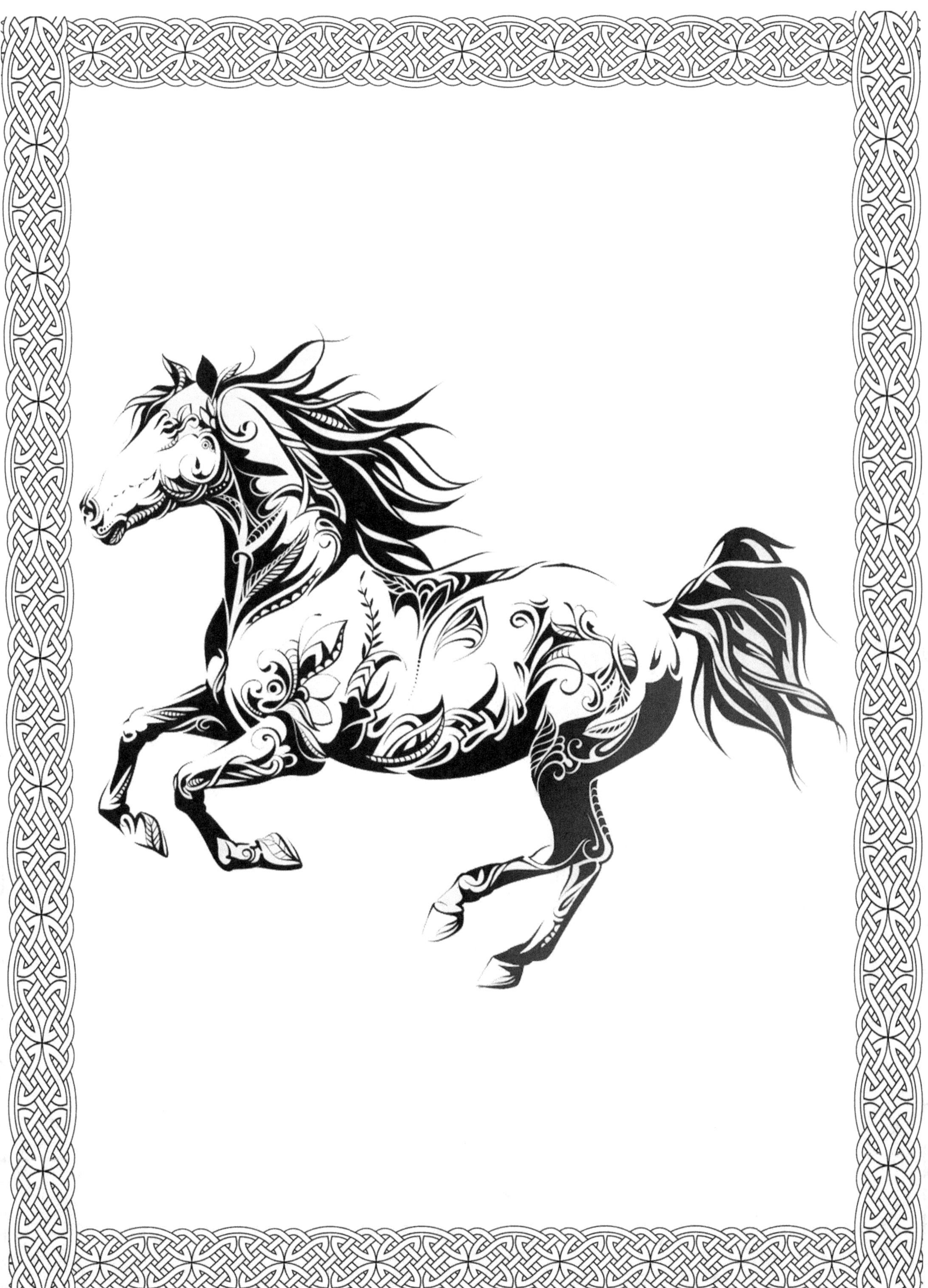

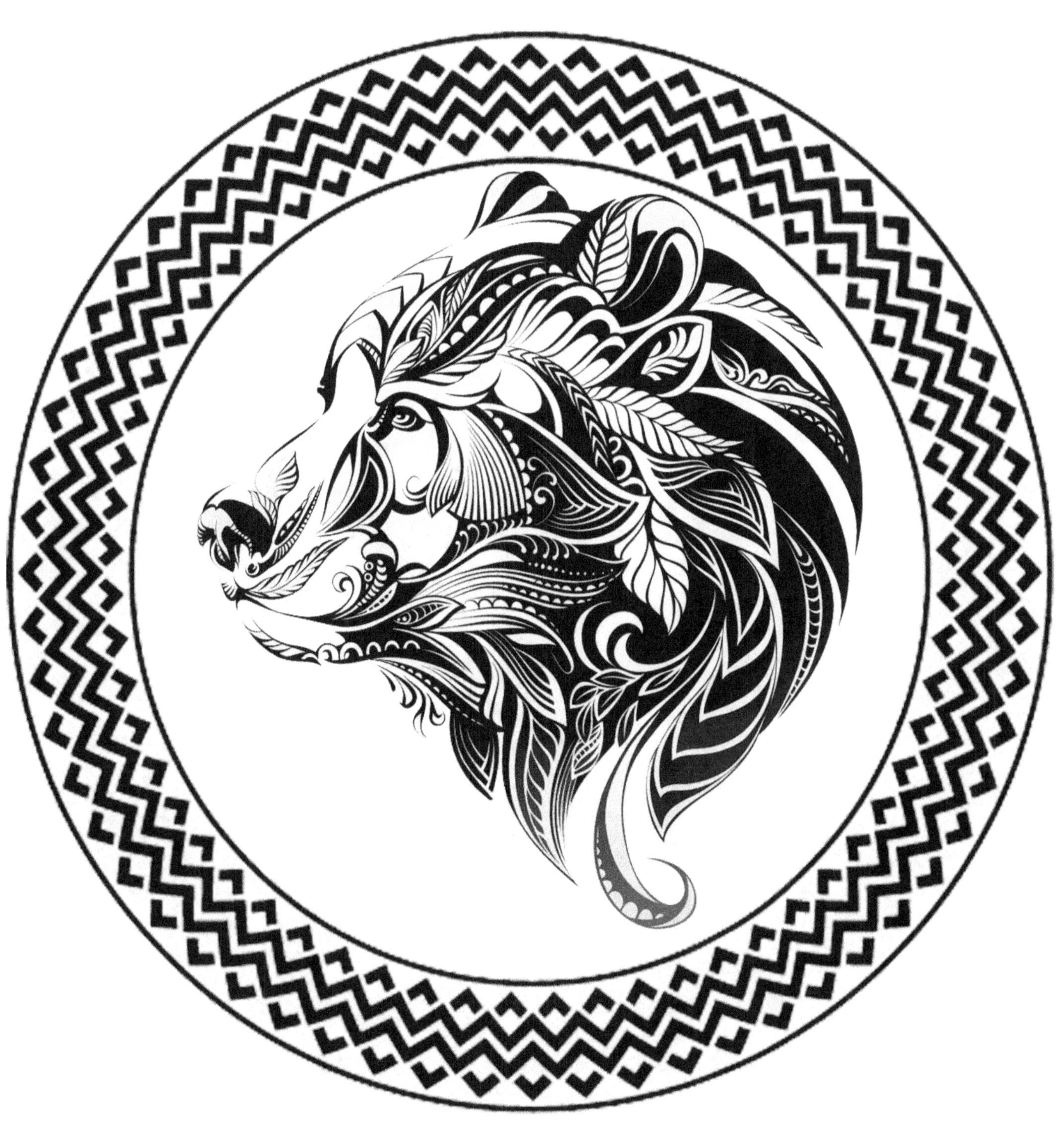

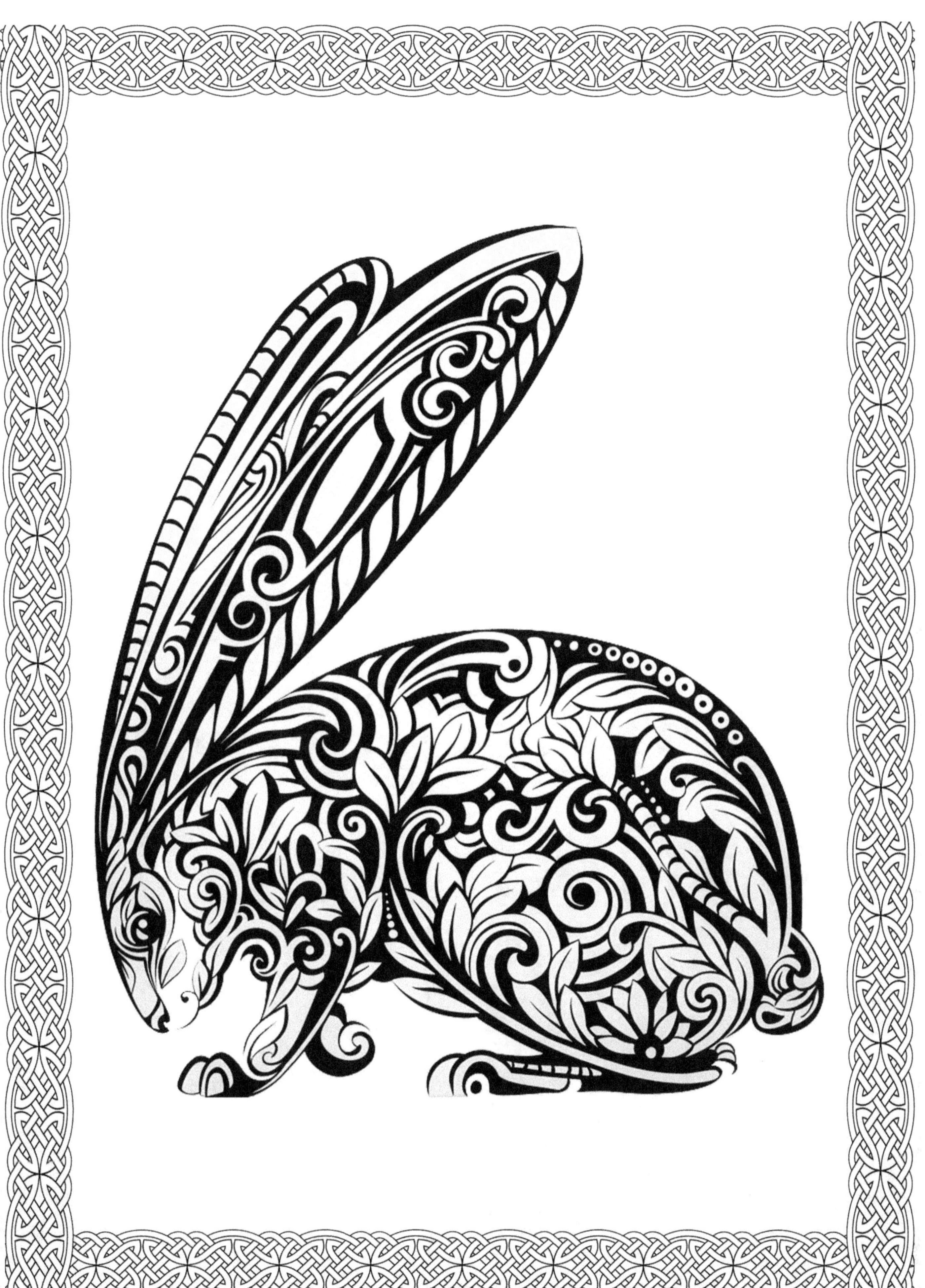

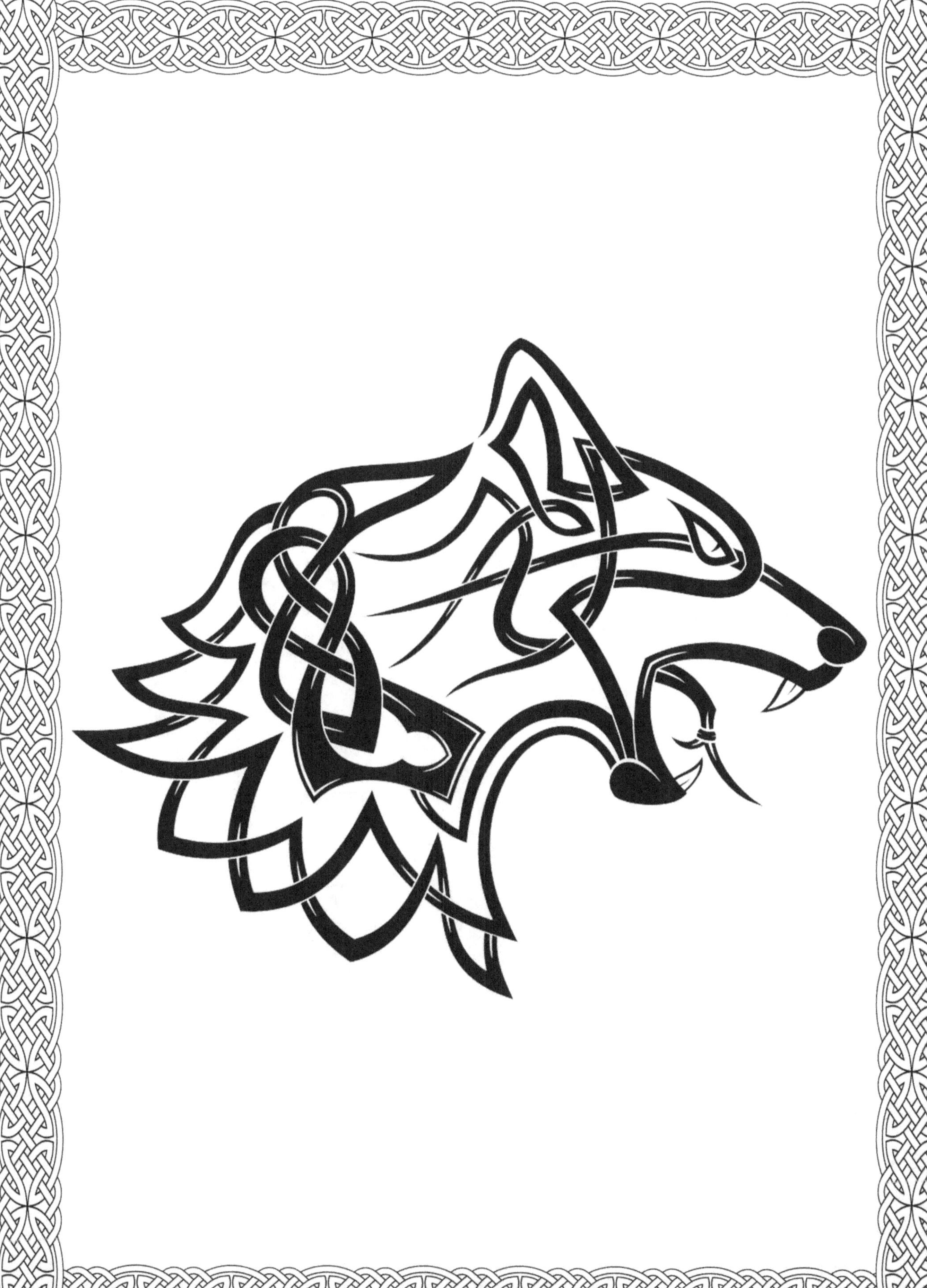

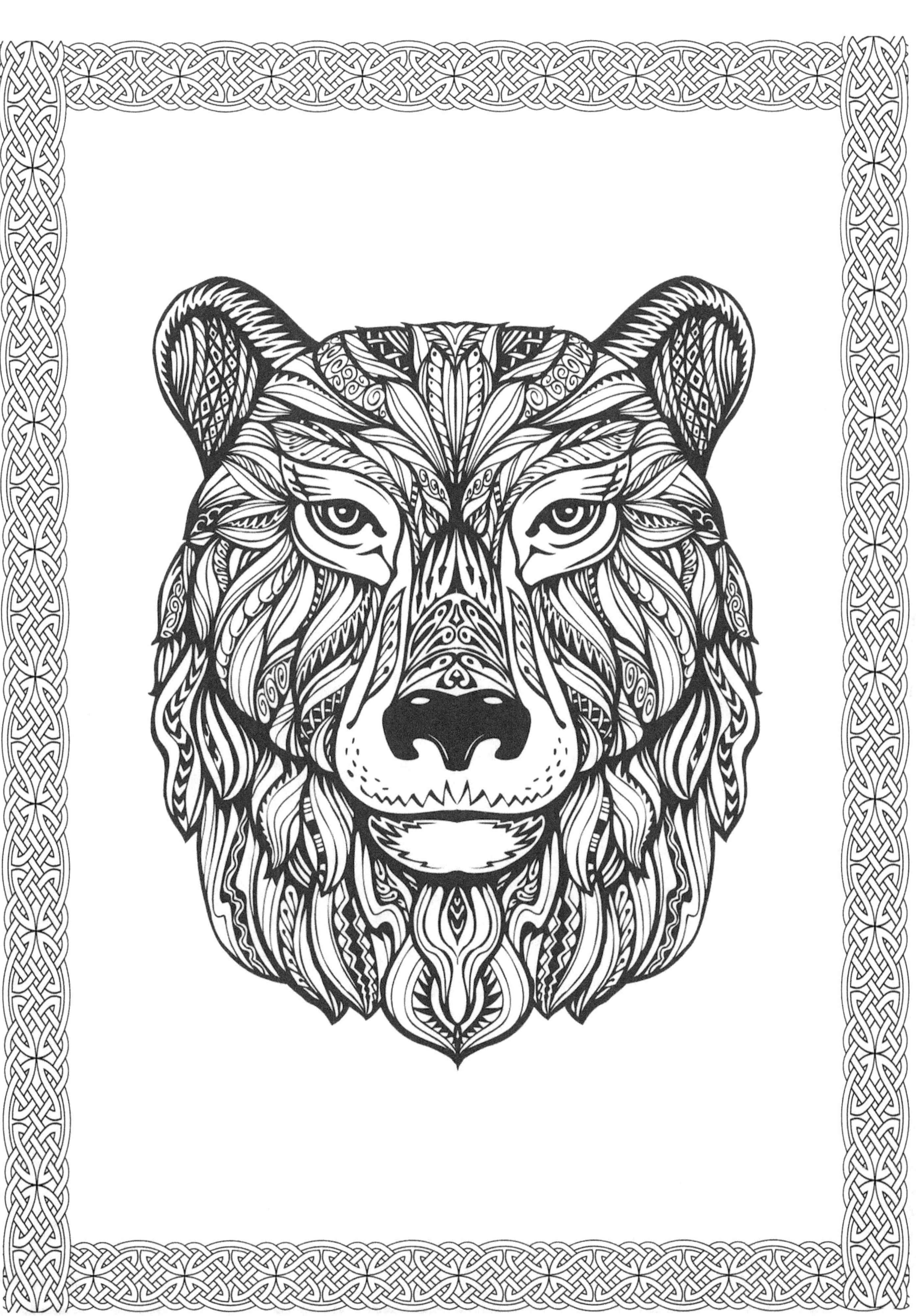

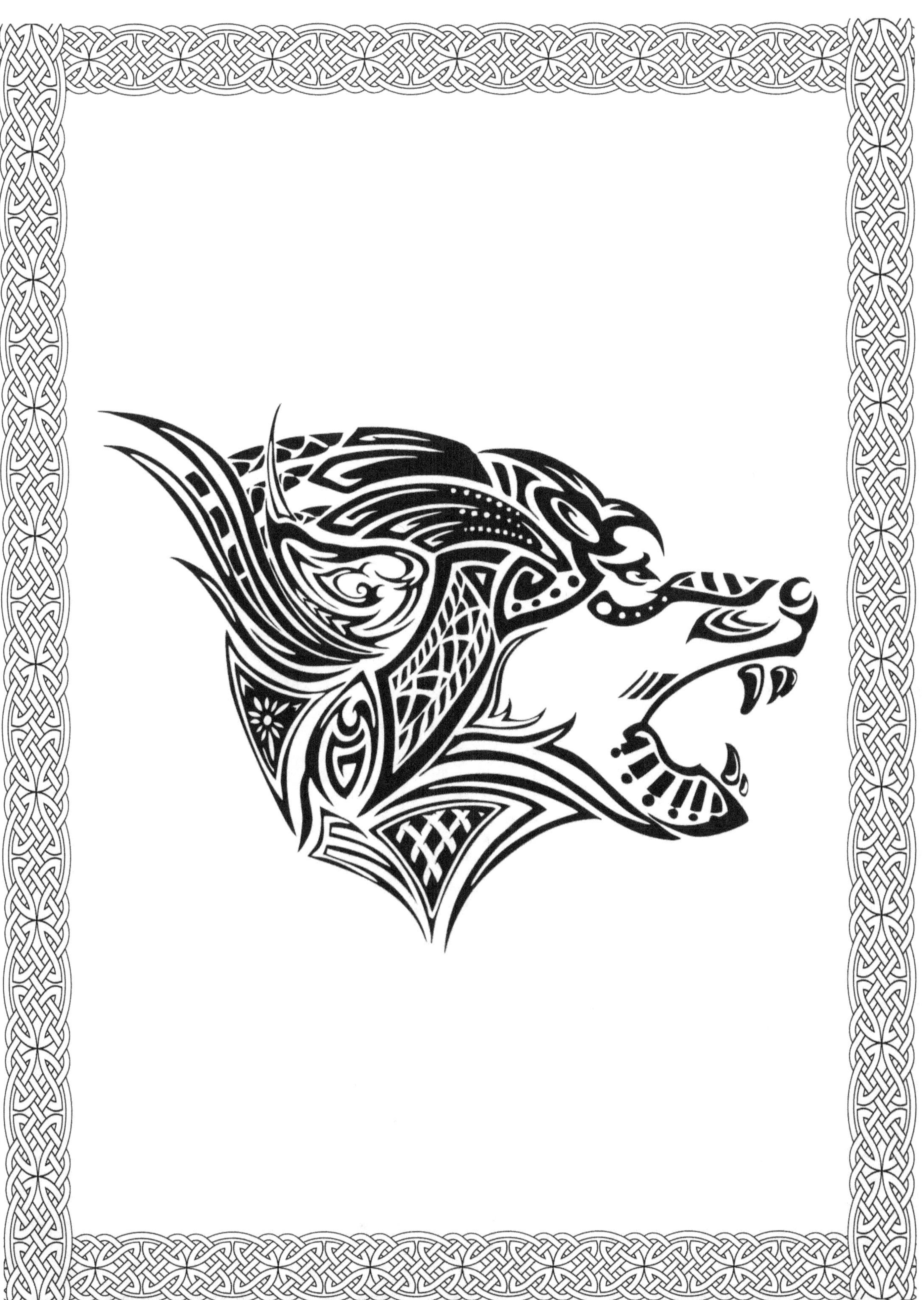

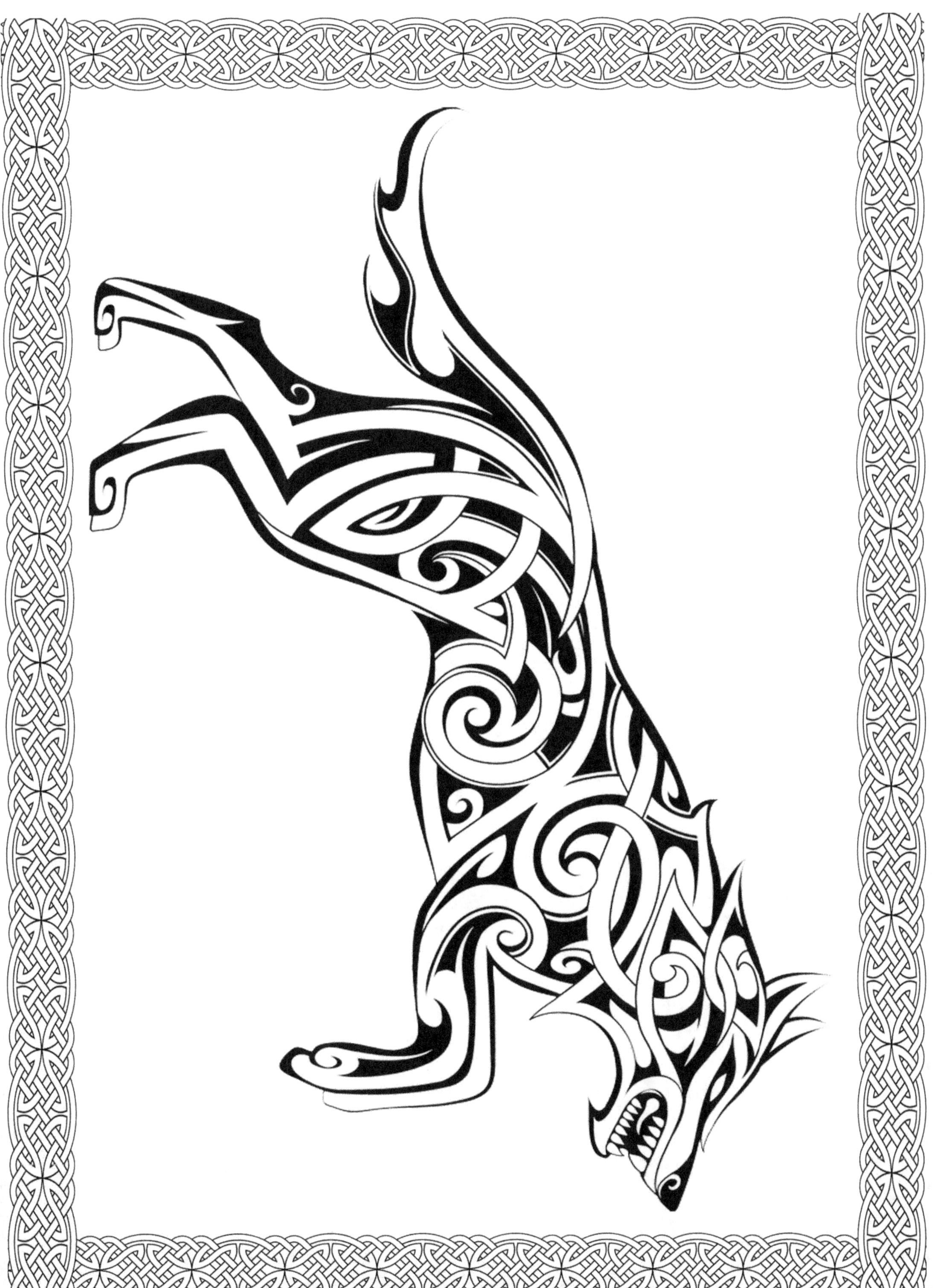

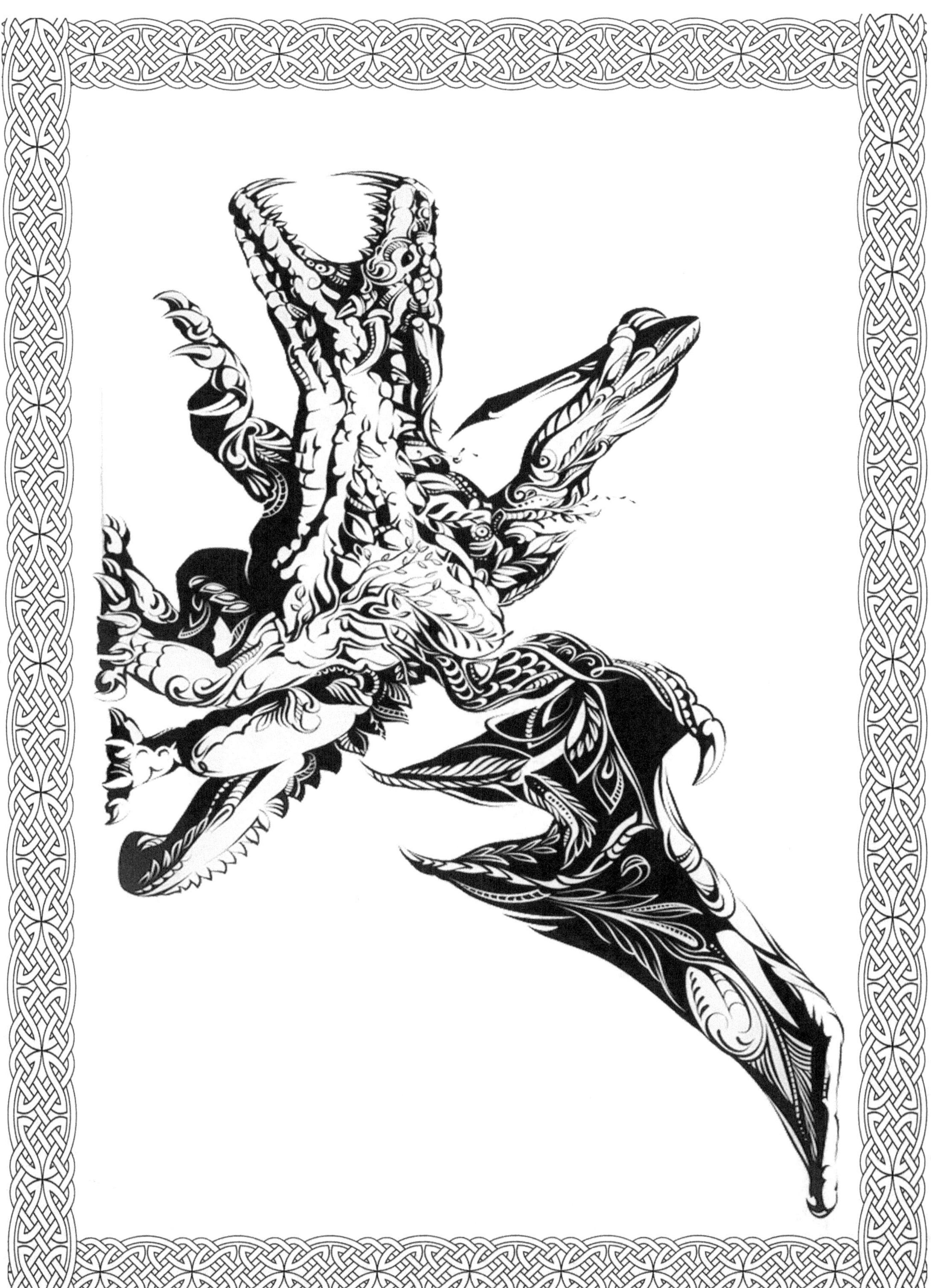

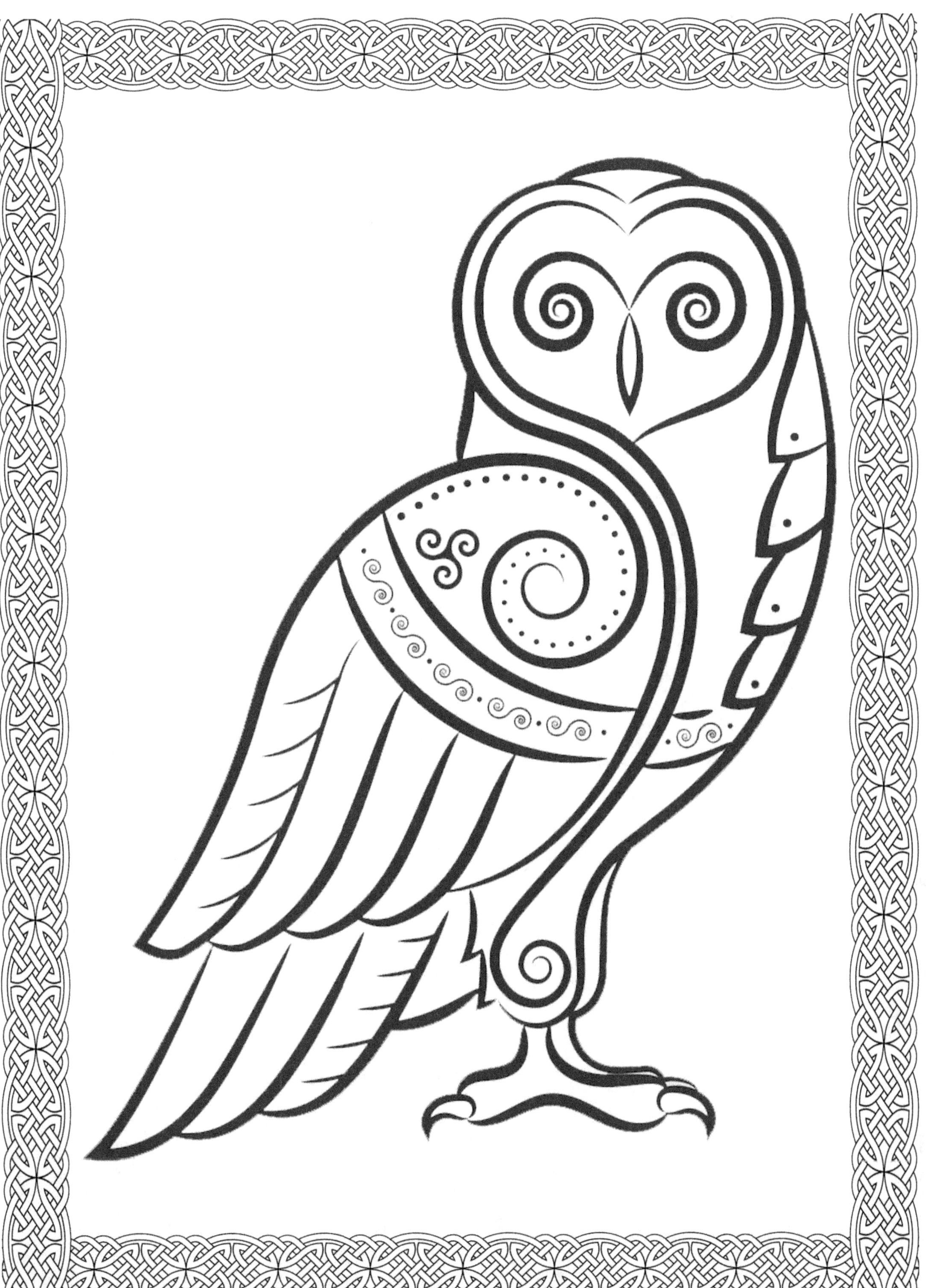

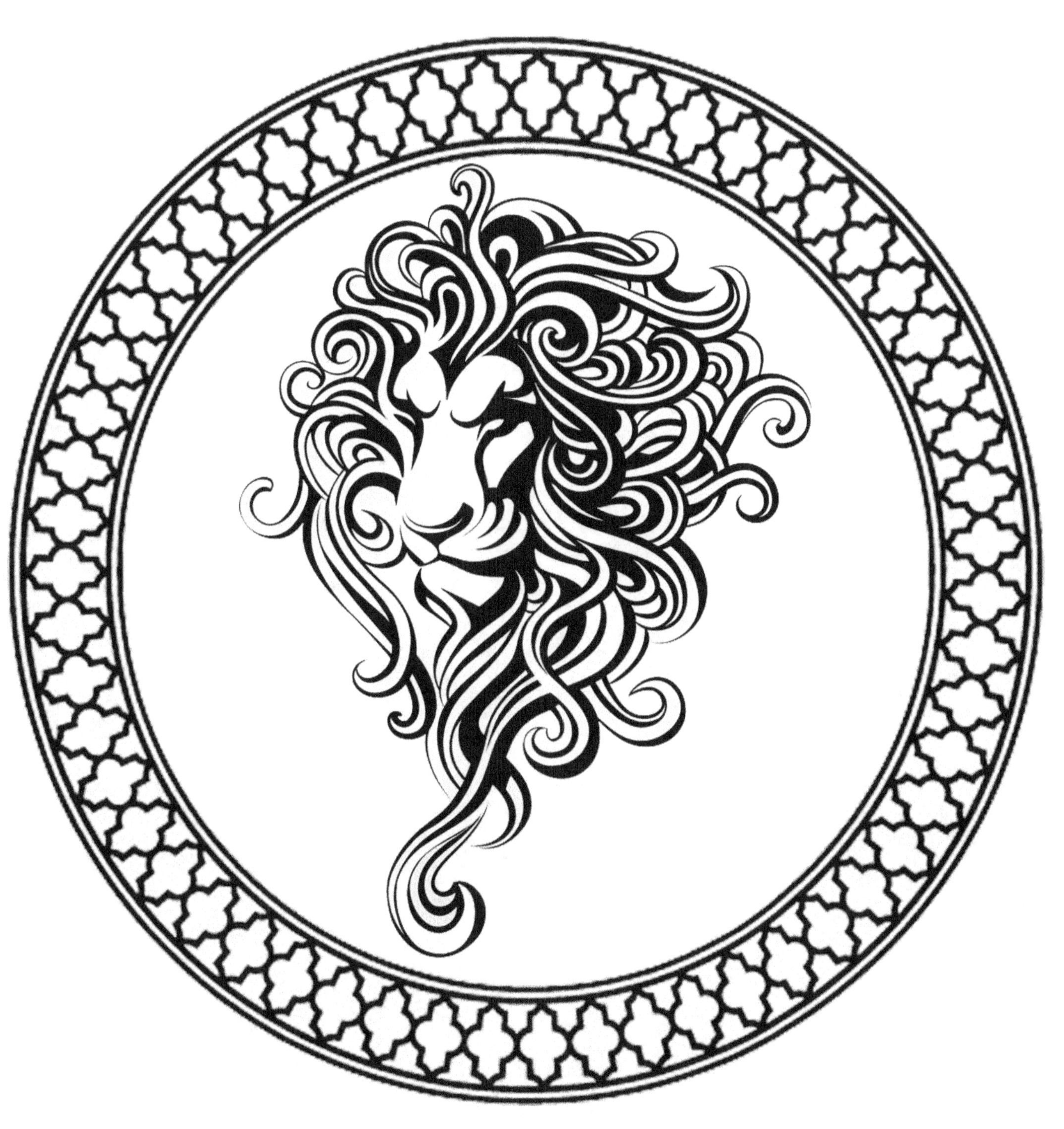

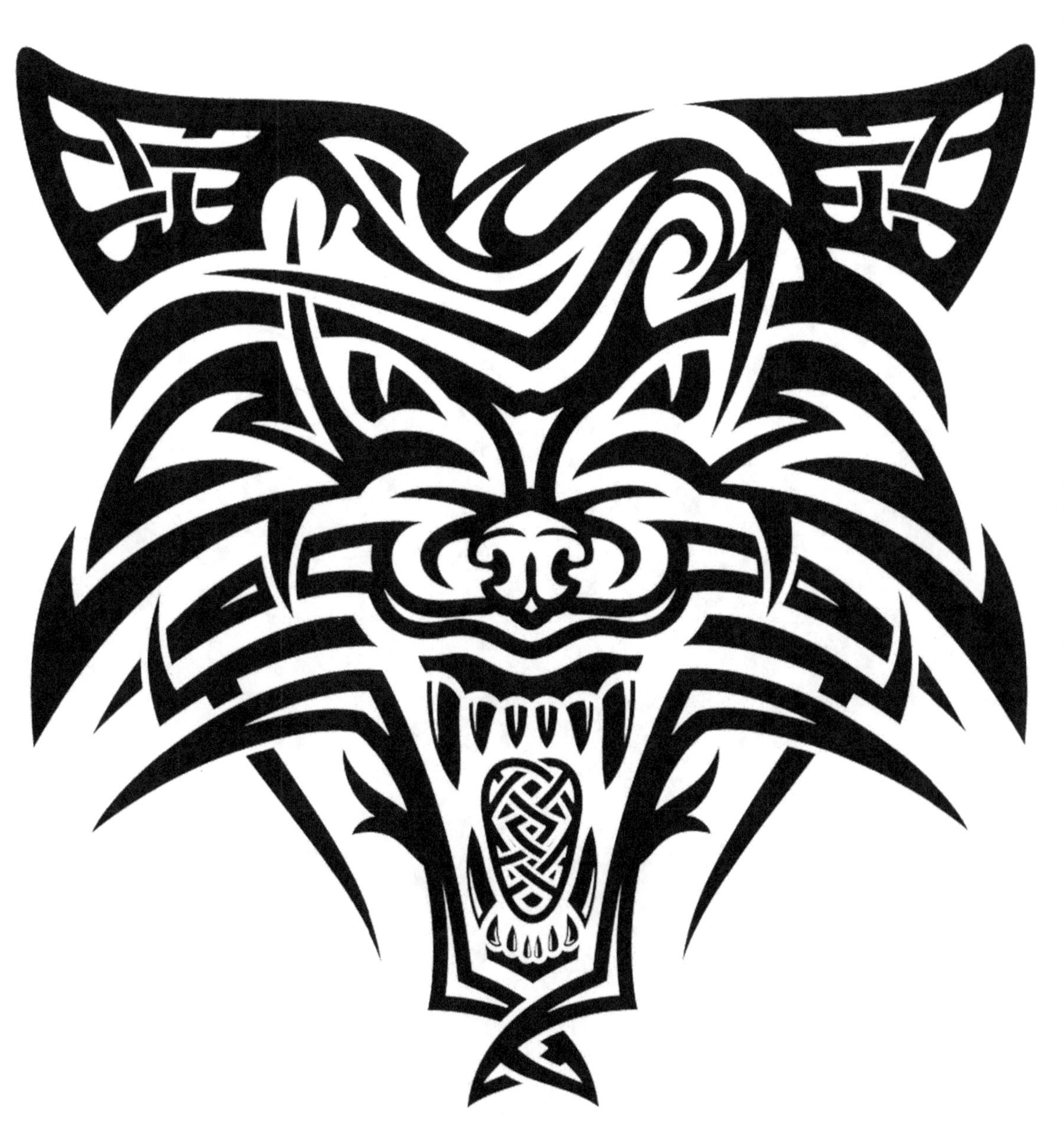

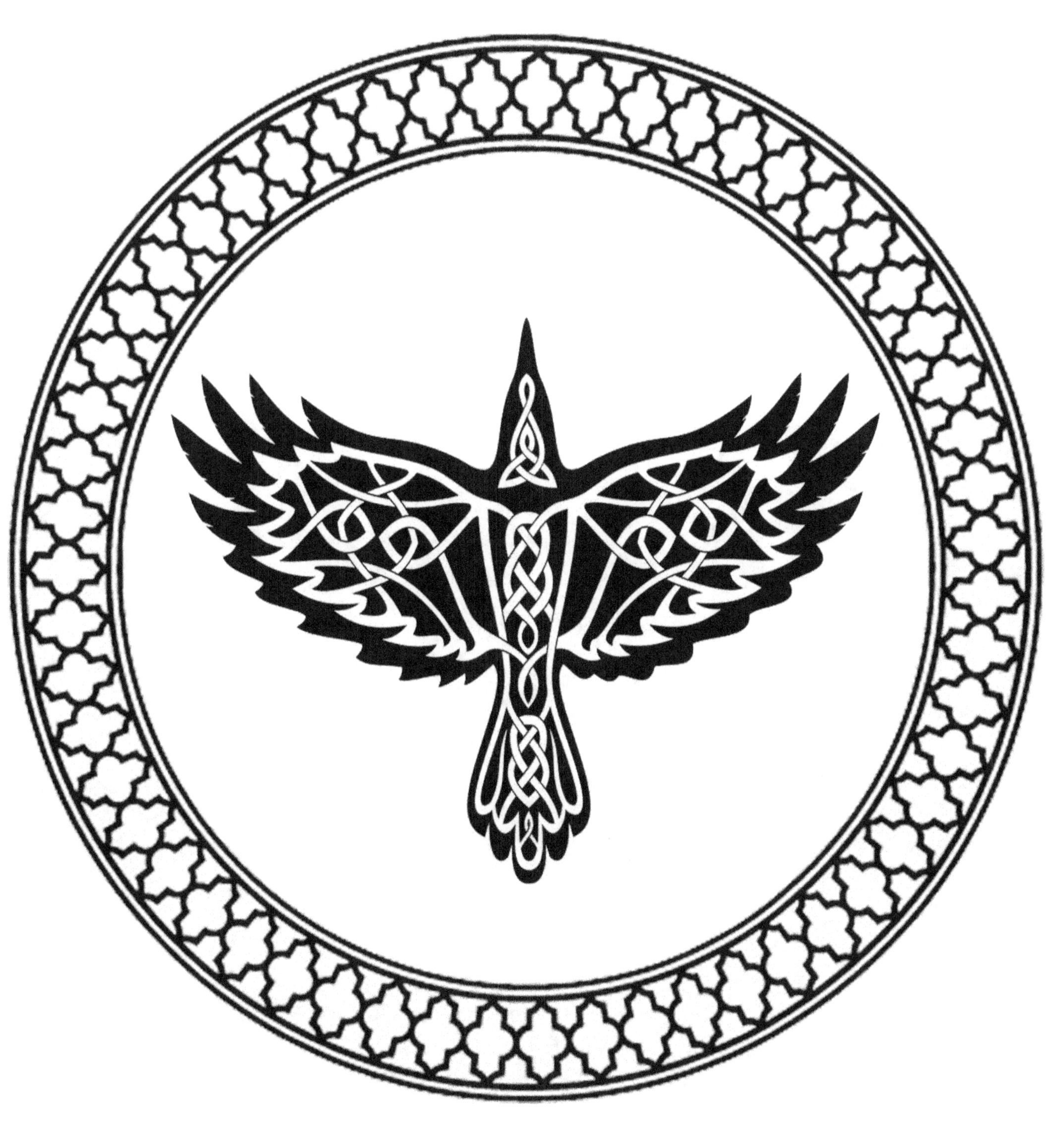

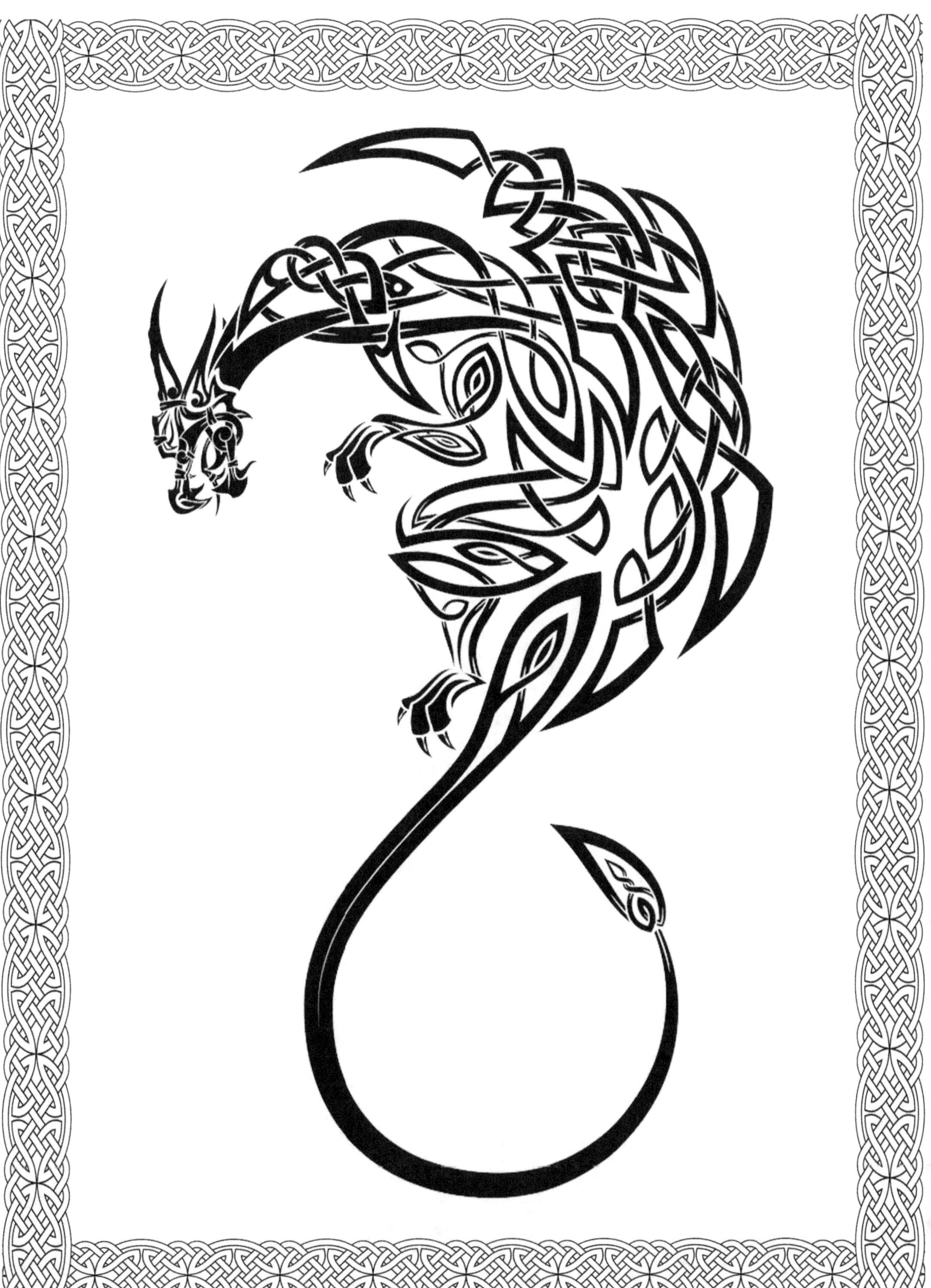

Found others coloring books

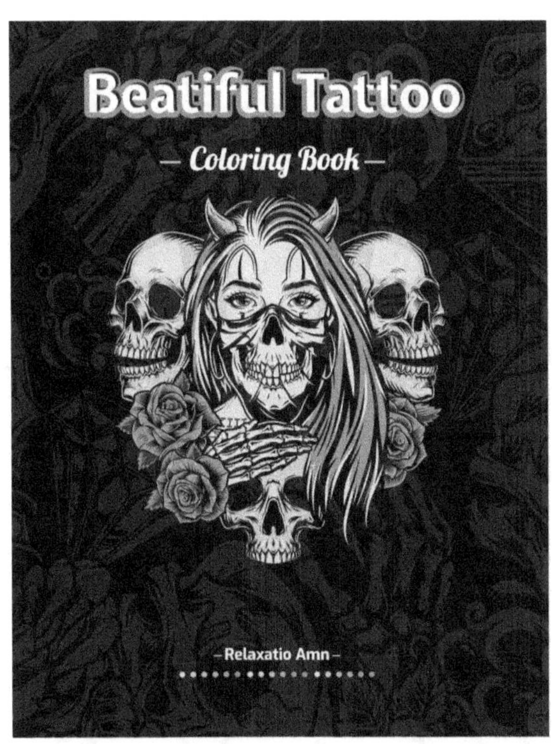

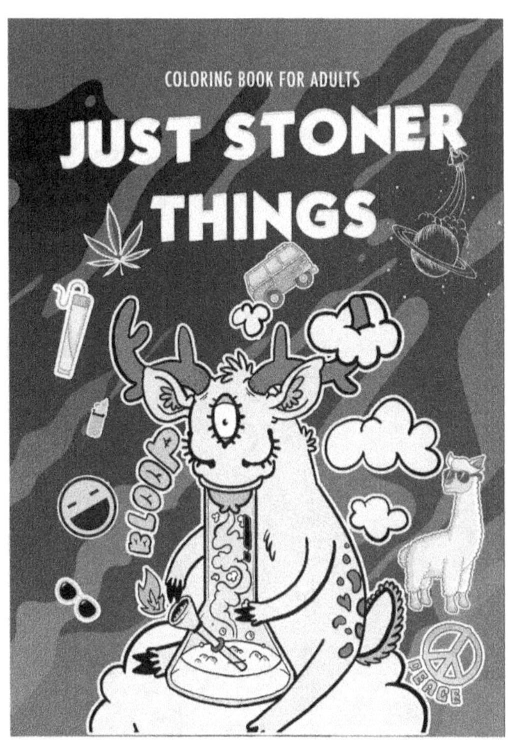

Relaxatio Amn